Pros and Cons

COMMUNICATION

The Impact of Science and Technology

Andrew Solway

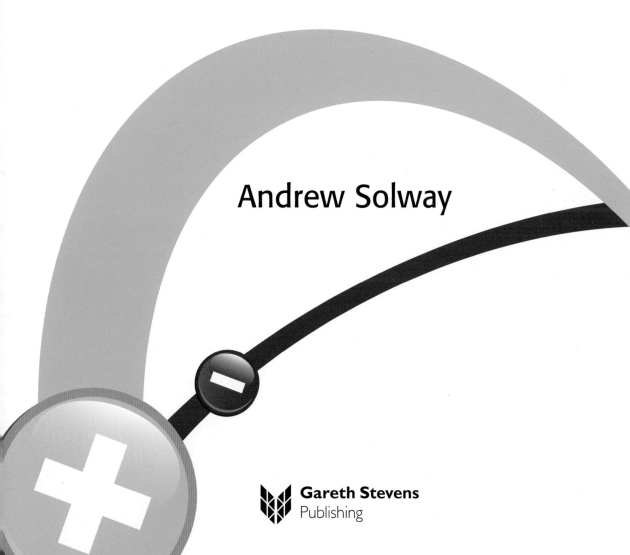

Gareth Stevens
Publishing

Please visit our web site at: www.garethstevens.com.
For a free color catalog describing Gareth Stevens Publishing's list of high-quality books, call 1-800-542-2595 (USA) or 1-800-387-3178 (Canada). Gareth Stevens Publishing's fax: 1-877-545-2596

Library of Congress Cataloging-in-Publication Data

Solway, Andrew.
    Communication : the impact of science and technology / by Andrew Solway.
       p. cm. — (Pros and cons)
    Includes bibliographical references and index.
    ISBN-13: 978-1-4339-1986-2 ISBN-10: 1-4339-1986-9   (lib. bdg.)
    1. Information technology—Juvenile literature.
    2. Telecommunication—Juvenile literature. 3. Communication—Juvenile literature. I. Title.
T58.5.S66   2010
303.48'33—dc22   2009012435

This North American edition published in 2010 by Gareth Stevens Publishing under license from Arcturus Publishing Limited.
Gareth Stevens Publishing
A Weekly Reader® Company
1 Reader's Digest Road
Pleasantville, NY 10570-7000 USA

Copyright © 2009 Arcturus Publishing Limited
Produced by Arcturus Publishing Limited
26/27 Bickels Yard
151-153 Bermondsey Street
London SE1 3HA

Gareth Stevens Executive Managing Editor: Lisa M. Herrington
Gareth Stevens Editor: Jayne Keedle
Gareth Stevens Senior Designer: Keith Plechaty

Series Concept: Alex Woolf
Editor and Picture Researcher: Nicola Barber
Cover Design: Phipps Design
Consultant: Bill Thompson

Picture Credits: Corbis: 7 (Leonard de Selva), 8, 13, 25 (Bettmann), 11 (Stefano Bianchetti), 17 (Jagadeesh/Reuters), 23 (George McNish/*The Star Ledger*), 27 (John Van Hasselt), 30 (Jose Luis Pelaez, Inc.), 34 (Gene Blevins), 37 (Najlah Feanny), 43 (Christian Charisius/Reuters), 45 (Heino Kalis/Reuters), 49 (B.S.P.I.), 52 (James Leynse), 57 (Andy Aitchison); Getty Images: 39 (Howard Kingsnorth); Science Photo Library: 5 (NASA/JPL), 19, 29, 46 (CERN), 54 (D. Roberts), 58 (David Parker); Shutterstock: Cover (Cristi Matei), 9 (Newton Page), 12 (Scott David Patterson), 16 (Eline Spek), 24 (Andrea Danti), 32 (Phillip Holland), 51 (Adrio Communications, Ltd).

Cover: A communications satellite orbits Earth.

Printed in the United States

1 2 3 4 5 6 7 8 9 15 14 13 12 11 10 09

CONTENTS

CHAPTER 1

Modern Communications

Teenager Rebecca Fyfe has good reason to be thankful for modern communications. When she and a group of friends found themselves drifting out of control on a damaged boat off the coast of Indonesia, they were unable to contact local rescue services. Rebecca texted her boyfriend, Nick, for help. Nick was in the United Kingdom — about 6,200 miles (9,978 kilometers) away! When he received her message, he alerted the U.K. coast guard, which notified rescue services in Indonesia. A ship was sent out, and eventually everyone was brought safely to shore.

Rebecca's text message was just one tiny part of the vast amount of information that we send around the world each day. Modern communications networks are so readily available that we almost take them for granted. The technology at the heart of all those networks is telecommunications.

Telecommunications

Telecommunication means "communication at a distance." All telecommunications systems have the same basic parts. First, the information to be sent is turned into a signal. A transmitter then sends that signal through a transmission medium, such as a wire, to one or more receivers. The receiver picks up the signal and turns it back into information.

In the modern world, there are many kinds of telecommunications systems. Whenever you make a phone call, listen to the radio, watch television, or use the Internet, you are using telecommunications. Police, firefighters, and ambulance crews use two-way radio links to communicate during emergencies. Businesses rely on e-mails and telephone calls

VIEWPOINT

Good Communication?

Advancements in communications technology have not always met with universal approval:

"The more elaborate our means of communication, the less we communicate."

(Joseph Priestley, 18th-century scientist and clergyman)

to correspond with their clients and one another. Banks rely on computers to transfer money around the world.

Since its launch in 1977, the *Voyager 1* space probe has continued to send radio signals back to its control center on Earth as it travels throughout the solar system.

 PROS: COMMUNICATIONS SYSTEMS

Good communications systems are an essential part of modern life, connecting people and businesses all over the world. Vast amounts of information can be transmitted instantly, and business transactions can be conducted in seconds. Today, it would be hard to imagine life without telephones, the Internet, televisions, or radios.

CONS: COMMUNICATIONS SYSTEMS

Communications systems can sometimes provide people with too much information. Many people use the Internet to learn about a particular topic. But researching a popular subject on the Internet can unearth far more information than it is possible to read. Looking up dinosaurs on Google, for example, produces links to more than 20 million web sites! Not all of those sites contain accurate information — and many of them simply sell products with a dinosaur theme.

Communications From the Past

Before the development of modern tele-communications systems, people used many other forms of communication. Visual signals were made with fires or with mirrors that reflected light from the sun. Sound signals were made with drums or with the human voice.

Printing made a huge difference in the communication of information. A German craftsman named Johannes Gutenberg developed a method of printing in the mid-1400s, and within 50 years that technique had spread across Europe. At first, printers made books that only a few people could afford. Then, in the early 1500s, printers began to produce pamphlets. Those booklets contained all kinds of information, ranging from the latest scientific discoveries to new religious ideas.

Whose Invention?

It is often said that Johannes Gutenberg did not invent printing. Since before Gutenberg's time, Koreans had already been printing books using individual bronze letters. But Gutenberg's printing process brought together several different ideas and improved on each one. His printing press applied pressure fast, so that pages could be printed quickly. Gutenberg invented new metal alloys with the right properties for making type. And he developed new inks that worked well in his printing press.

PROS: NEW TECHNOLOGIES

The improved communication that resulted from the development of printing had far-reaching effects. Many more books could be produced. They were still very expensive, but printers also produced pamphlets and newspapers that almost anyone could afford. Suddenly, people had access to information and new ideas they never had before.

CONS: NEW TECHNOLOGIES

New technology often leads to the loss of earlier forms of communication. The printing press, for example, replaced the skilled calligraphers and illustrators who created the beautiful, handmade books of the Middle Ages. Similarly, the development of the Internet and other electronic forms of information is threatening the dominance of printed books and newspapers today.

Semaphore

In the early 1790s, French brothers Claude and Ignace Chappe developed what was perhaps the first real telecommunications technology — a signaling system called semaphore. The Chappes built a series of towers. On top of each tower was a long bar, with two shorter "arms" that were positioned in different ways to indicate different letters or words. Information was passed from place to place rapidly along the line of towers. Semaphore spread across Europe and to the United States, though it was mainly used for military communications. By the 1830s, the system was being replaced by the electric telegraph.

This illustration shows one of the semaphore signaling towers designed in the 1790s by Claude and Ignace Chappe. A second tower can be seen in the distance (*far right*), and the man on the right is reading its signal using a telescope.

CHAPTER 2

Cables and Signals

The electric telegraph is sometimes called the Victorian Internet. More than a century before the World Wide Web or communications satellites, the telegraph system was sending messages around the world. It was the earliest form of electric telecommunications.

The first successful electric telegraph was developed by two British inventors, William Cooke and Charles Wheatstone, in 1837. It used six wires and a set of five needles, each of which could be made to move left or right to point to letters on a display. Although the needle telegraph was successful for a time, the equipment was complicated and expensive. It was soon replaced by an improved system from the United States. Samuel Morse and his assistant, Alfred Vail, invented a telegraph that used only one wire and worked by sending messages in code. The code became known as Morse code,

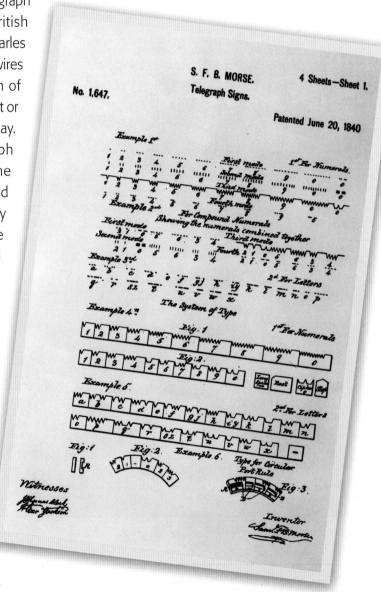

A patent gives inventors legal ownership of their inventions. This is part of the original patent documents for Morse code. It shows the dots and dashes that make up the telegraph signs.

Morse Code

Morse code translated each letter into a pattern of dots and dashes. Those were sent using a telegraph key, which was simply a switch that sprang open when it was let go. The operator sent a dot by holding the key down very briefly and a dash by holding it down slightly longer. At the other end of the wire, a printer recorded a black mark on a strip of paper whenever an electric pulse came through the wire. A dot was a short mark, while a dash was longer. Telegraph operators quickly learned to "read" a Morse code message by listening to the pattern of clicks the telegraph made as a message came through. An experienced operator could send and receive messages very quickly.

though Vail developed it with Morse. The Morse telegraph was cheap and easy to use. The first Morse telegraph link was set up between Washington, D.C., and Baltimore, Maryland, in 1844. Within a few years, Morse's telegraph was being used in countries around the world.

A telegraph key was used for tapping Morse code. Experienced operators understood messages from the sound of the taps, without having to look at the final printout.

Telegraph Beats Train

By the 1850s, many countries had a telegraph service of some kind. Newspaper reporters used the telegraph to send in their latest stories. Police found that it could be useful for catching criminals. In 1845, a woman named Sarah Hart was found dead from poisoning in her cottage in Slough, a town west of London. Suspicion soon fell on John Tawell, who had visited her that morning. The police learned that Tawell was on a train from Slough to London's Paddington Station. They telegraphed ahead to Paddington, and Tawell was arrested when he got off the train. It was the first time the telegraph was used to catch a murderer.

Transatlantic Links

In 1866, the SS *Great Eastern*, at that time the biggest ship in the world, laid a telegraph cable across the Atlantic Ocean connecting North America and England. Soon, there were connections between every continent. In 1885, more than 33 million telegraph messages were sent. By 1900, that number had risen to 90 million. The telephone was invented in 1876, and it soon replaced the telegraph for some communications. However, telegraph remained the only global communications network until 1927, when the first radiotelephone link was made across the Atlantic.

 PROS: ELECTRIC TELEGRAPH

The electric telegraph was extremely successful. The speed of communications provided by telegraph made an enormous impact on society. Together with the railroad, telegraphs influenced a transition to a faster-paced society.

 CONS: ELECTRIC TELEGRAPH

Telegraphs were limited in the information they could send. Most people could not send their own messages. Until after 1900, most telegraphs used only Morse code. That meant that skilled operators were needed to send and receive messages. Only rich people and businesses could afford their own telegraph equipment; others had to use a public telegraph office. Private messages were further encoded to keep them secret.

"Mr. Watson, Come Here ..."

In 1876, Alexander Graham Bell was trying out his latest design for a "speaking telegraph." He had been working on the idea for several years with his assistant, Thomas Watson. Speaking into the apparatus of his invention, Bell said to Watson, who was in another room, "Mr. Watson, come here — I want to see you." That was the first telephone call. A new telecommunications revolution had begun.

The first few years of telephone history involved patent battles over who had the right to manufacture telephones. One large manufacturing company made telephones to the design of an American engineer named Elisha Gray for Western Union Telegraph Company. American inventor Thomas Edison developed a microphone for the telephone that worked better than Bell's. There were more than 600 court cases challenging Bell as the inventor of the telephone. However, Bell's company won them all.

An Impractical Device?

VIEWPOINT

In 1876, Alexander Graham Bell and his financial backer, Gardiner Hubbard, offered the telephone patent to the Western Union Telegraph Company. This excerpt was taken from a report made by a committee that reviewed that offer:

"Technically, we do not see that this device [the telephone] will be ever capable of sending recognizable speech over a distance of several miles .... Furthermore, why would any person want to use this ungainly and impractical device when he can ... have a clear written message sent to any large city in the United States?"

The first long-distance call was made in 1876. By 1892, long-distance telephone service began from New York to Chicago.

Communicating Through Cables

The first telephones used a single steel wire, like the telegraph system did. However, there was much more interference with the telephone signal than with a telegraph signal. Using two wires instead of one made some improvement. Another problem was that telephone signals could not travel far along steel wires. Experiments using different metals showed that signals traveled much farther along copper wires.

Even with the cables sorted out, there was still a problem with long-distance calls. The signal got weaker gradually. Then, in the early 1900s, the first amplifiers were developed. An amplifier is a device that boosts an electrical signal. By adding amplifiers at intervals, it became possible to send telephone signals thousands of miles.

How a Telephone Works

A telephone transmitter (the mouthpiece) turns sound into electrical signals, and the receiver (the earpiece) turns those signals back into sound. Thomas Edison invented the most widely used transmitter, the carbon microphone. Speaking into the microphone causes a thin metal plate, called a diaphragm, to vibrate. The vibrations of the plate produce a varying electrical current, or electrical signal. The signal is sent through the telephone wires to a receiver. The telephone receiver is a small loudspeaker. The changing electric current produces a changing magnetic field in a coil of wire. The coil pulls and pushes on another magnet, which is attached to a diaphragm. That movement cause the diaphragm to vibrate, and those vibrations create sounds.

Early telephones had a bell (*top*), a mouthpiece (*middle*), and an earpiece (*left*). Early phones did not have an electricity supply. The caller turned the handle (*right*), which activated a small generator, producing the electricity that powered the phone.

Connecting People

An essential part of the telephone network was the telephone exchange. From the start, all telephone lines from a local area were connected to a central exchange. In early exchanges, the calls were connected by human operators. That changed in 1891 with an invention made by an American funeral director named Almon Strowger. Strowger was convinced that an operator in his local exchange was putting through callers to a rival company. To stop that from happening, he invented a system that connected calls automatically. Callers dialed a series of numbers, each of which sent electric pulses down the telephone line to the exchange. The electric pulses moved switches on a selector. Once the final number was dialed, the exchange connected the caller to the phone identified by that number.

Below is a New York telephone exchange as it appeared in 1897. By that year, millions of people had telephones. Each call had to be connected by hand by a human operator.

PROS: EARLY PHONES

In most ways, the telephone was a great improvement on the telegraph. For the first time, people could talk to one another directly over long distances. Although the telephone was expensive at first, it soon became affordable. By 1900, there were more than 3 million telephones in the United States.

CONS: EARLY PHONES

Early telephone systems had poor sound quality, especially over long distances. For many years, telephone networks did not extend worldwide in the same way the telegraph did. A telephone call did not produce a written record. That meant that it was not useful for sending detailed information. For businesses in particular, the telephone was a useful addition, but it did not immediately replace the telegraph.

Going Digital

In 1937, a British engineer named Alex Reeves was looking for a way to cut out the background noise that plagued many telephone calls. Interference from other calls or from

Analog Versus Digital

The electrical signal produced by a telephone transmitter is continuously changing. Any electrical signal that changes continuously is analog. A digital signal changes in sudden steps or jumps. That is because digital signals are made up of thousands of samples, or measurements, of an analog signal. Each digital sample has a specific value. For example, it might have a value of 2 at one point and 4 a moment later.

To transmit a digital signal, each sample number is converted into a binary number. Binary is a numbering system that uses only the numbers 0 and 1. For example, the number 2 becomes 10 in binary code, while 4 becomes 100. In this way, the analog signal is turned into a long string of 1s and 0s. It can be transmitted as an electrical signal with just two values.

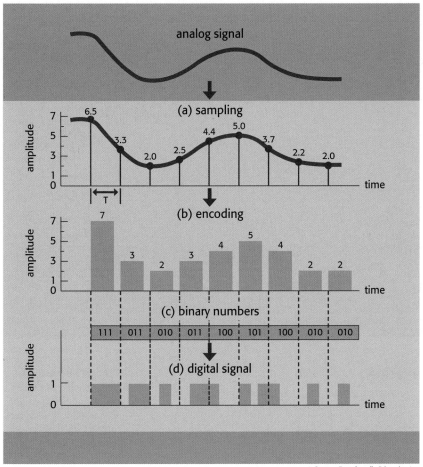

This diagram shows how an analog signal, one second in length, is turned into a digital one. The first stage is to sample the analog signal (a). That means measuring it at regular intervals ("T" on the graph). The analog signal is sampled many times per second. For conversion to a digital signal, the values for each sample are rounded up or down (b), then converted to binary numbers (c). Those can be turned into a string of "on" and "off" pulses — a digital signal (d).

Source: Encyclopedia Britannica, Inc.

electrical equipment could cause all kinds of whistles, hisses, and howls. Reeves came up with the idea of turning the continuous electrical signal into a string of electric pulses. He called his idea pulse-code modulation (PCM). Reeves's system turned an analog telephone signal, which is a signal that changes smoothly and continuously, into a digital one.

A digital signal changes in small steps rather than continuously and can be written as a string of binary code, which uses only the numbers 0 and 1. The great advantage of a digital signal is that because each point in the signal can have only value 0 or value 1, it is much easier to copy it exactly. Little noise or interference can obscure the difference between a 0 or a 1. However, the first digital telephone exchanges were not set up until the 1970s, when microchips and computers made the technology easier to use and much less expensive.

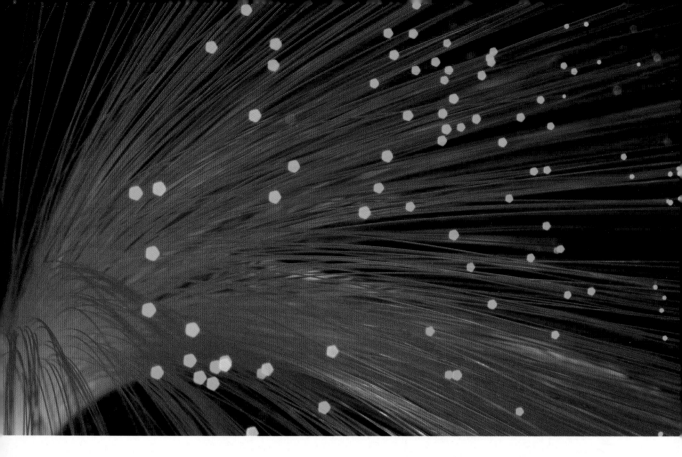

Fitting In More Information

As telephones became more popular, it became difficult to provide enough lines for everyone who wanted to make calls. Engineers came up with several ways to send more than one call down the same line. One way of combining calls was known as time-division multiplexing. That involved breaking each telephone call into small sections, or packets. A packet from one telephone call was sent down the line, followed by a packet from a second telephone call, and so on. The packets were joined again at the other end of the line.

In the 1970s, optical fibers added extra capacity to telephone lines. The thin, flexible strands of glass carried information using laser light rather than electricity. They could carry 65,000 times more information than a similar copper wire could.

Optical fibers carry information as pulses of laser light. The light can travel long distances along thin glass or plastic cables.

Telephone Signals By Radio

When radio was developed in the early 1900s, it became possible to send telephone calls as radio signals rather than by wires. That worked best for long-distance calls that were difficult to make via cables, such as those that crossed oceans. The first radiotelephone call across the Atlantic Ocean was made between New York City and London in 1927.

PROS: DIALING LONG DISTANCE

Improvements in telephone technology mean that you can now dial direct to anywhere in the world. The sound quality of intercontinental calls is almost as good as that of local calls. The low cost of long-distance calls has allowed some businesses to save money by establishing their call centers in other countries where labor costs are lower. Call centers that deal with customers' questions are easy to outsource. Often, people with questions about a Western company's product find their queries are answered by call center staff in India.

CONS: DIALING LONG DISTANCE

Telephone calls are often used as a way to sell products. Most people find such telemarketing very annoying. In some cases, the products or services are scams. In one case, con artists in the United States phoned elderly people in the United Kingdom and persuaded them to buy shares in companies that turned out not to exist.

Outsourcing cuts costs for businesses, but it is often unpopular with their customers. Moving call centers abroad takes jobs away from the company's home country. Also, call centers located overseas can be frustrating for customers, who might struggle to understand foreign accents.

Many companies have overseas call centers, where people answer telephone calls from customers who have questions or complaints. Using modern communications, a call center can be thousands of miles away from the customer. Many call centers for U.S. companies are in India.

CHAPTER 3

Radio

An old-fashioned name for a radio is a wireless. That name explains clearly the difference between early telephones and early radios. Telephones needed wires for communication, but radios did not. Instead, radio transmissions relied on radio waves, which are a type of electromagnetic radiation.

At first, radios were used to communicate between two people, like telephones. Later, they were also used for broadcasting — sending out radio signals that many people could receive at once. The first radio signals carried Morse code dots and dashes, but they quickly began to carry sound messages. Today, radio signals can carry a wide variety of communications — text messages, telephone calls, televison programs, or information from the Internet, for example.

Electromagnetic Radiation

Radio waves are one type of electromagnetic radiation, but there are many other kinds, each with a different wavelength and energy. Radio waves are long-wavelength, low-energy waves. At the other end of the scale are gamma rays and cosmic rays, which have very short wavelengths and high-energy waves. All the different types of electromagnetic radiation move at the speed of light. Generally, they travel in a straight line, but, like light, all electromagnetic waves can be reflected and refracted, or bent.

Signaling With Radio Waves

Radio waves were first discovered in 1886 by German physicist Heinrich Hertz. Hertz thought that the invisible waves would be of little use for communications. They traveled only a few feet, and if he placed the transmitters too close together, they interfered with one another and hissed. But within a few years of the discovery of radio waves, Italian physicist Guglielmo Marconi proved Hertz wrong. He developed a radio telegraph that was like a Morse telegraph, but without wires.

Marconi realized that radio was ideal for communications on the move. He persuaded several shipping companies to try out his radio equipment. In 1899, a coal ship called the *RF Matthews* crashed into the *East Goodwin* lightship off the coast of southeast England. The lightship was fitted with a radio and sent a distress message in Morse code to the shore. Lifeboats were sent to help in the first of many sea rescues made possible by radio communication.

The First Broadcast

Meanwhile, a Canadian engineer named Reginald Fessenden was working on a radio system that could send continuous sounds. Fessenden produced a powerful wave, called a carrier wave. He added a sound signal to this carrier wave and transmited the combined signal. At the receiving end, the carrier wave was separated from the sound signal, which was then played through headphones or a loudspeaker. That is the way radio works today. Fessenden made the first radio broadcast on Christmas Eve in 1906 from the coast of Massachusetts. That broadcast was heard by radio operators on ships far out at sea. A second broadcast, on New Year's Eve, reached as far as the West Indies.

Better Radios

In 1905, an American inventor, Lee de Forest, created a device called an audion, or triode. It was a glass bulb, similar to a lightbulb, that could be used to amplify radio signals, making them stronger. Before, radio signals could be heard only through headphones. Now, the amplified signal could power a loudspeaker.

During World War I (1914–1918), governments in the United States and Europe banned all private radio transmissions. They wanted to keep

AM and FM Radio

Adding a sound signal to a carrier wave is known as modulation. In early radio, the sound signal modified the carrier wave by changing its amplitude, which is the height of each wave. That is called amplitude modulation, or AM. In 1933, an American engineer named Edwin Armstrong announced the invention of frequency modulation (FM). In FM, the sound signal changes the carrier wave's frequency, which is the number of waves produced per second. The advantage of FM radio is that it is far less affected by interference than AM radio is.

This diagram shows how radio signals are formed. In AM radio (a), the sound signal (the modulating wave) changes the amplitude, or height, of the carrier wave. In FM radio (b), the sound signal changes the frequency of the carrier wave by changing the distance between waves.

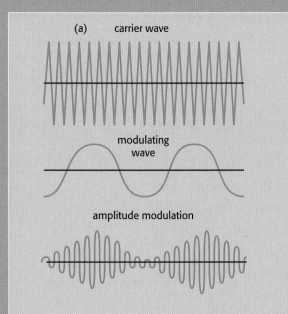
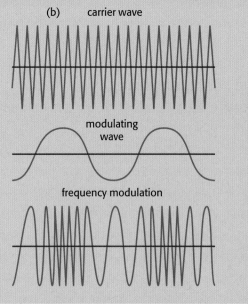

(a) carrier wave

modulating wave

amplitude modulation

(b) carrier wave

modulating wave

frequency modulation

Source: Computer Desktop Encyclopedia, 2007

the airwaves free for vital military communications. For the first time, soldiers on battlefields used radios to communicate with their commanders at headquarters. After the war ended, national radio broadcasts began in both the United States and Europe.

Radios were used very differently in World War II (1939–1945). By then, most people had radios in their homes, so national broadcasts were used to keep ordinary people informed of what was happening. A new problem with military communications was the ability to tune in to the enemy's radio messages. Important messages had to be coded to keep them secret. Soon, both sides were busy breaking each other's codes, and an "information war" began alongside the war on the ground.

Solid State Electronics

After World War II, radios became smaller and had no moving parts. Those electrical components are called solid state. A new kind of amplifier called a transistor replaced the triode. Triodes were the size of lightbulbs, whereas transistors were the size of peas. By the 1960s, transistor radios were inexpensive and pocket-sized. They were one of the reasons why rock-and-roll music became popular. People heard the music on the radio, then bought records of their favorite artists.

 PROS: RADIO TECHNOLOGY

Radios do not require wires or poles to carry their signals. As a result, one of the first uses of radios was to communicate to and from places that weren't reachable by telephone, such as from ship to shore. Radios were soon also being used by the armed forces, police, and ambulance and fire services to communicate emergency instructions.

 CONS: RADIO TECHNOLOGY

It is more difficult to keep radio signals free from interference than it is for telephone signals. Radio transmissions can also be intercepted by anyone with the right equipment.

Separating Signals

Many different carrier waves are used to transmit radio signals. Those carrier waves each work at a different frequency, in order not to interfere with one another. The radio wave spectrum is divided into many different frequency ranges, called wave bands, each of which can carry a different signal. The bandwidth, or size of a wave band, depends on the amount of information it has to carry. A music radio station, for example, needs a large bandwidth.

In today's world, radio wave bands are very crowded. They are used to carry radio programs, military radio, rescue service communications, TV signals, Internet links — even baby monitors. There are strict rules, made by the International Telecommunication Union, about which wave bands can be used for what purposes. Without those rules, television and radio broadcasts, phone calls, police radio, and other transmissions would all interfere with one another and cause chaos.

Radio Audiences

Before television, national radio stations had huge audiences. That was because there were few radio stations and no other competing media. Today, many radio broadcasters are moving to digital broadcasts. Digital radio transmissions can be compressed, which makes it possible to have a large number of digital radio stations. However, that also means that each station has a relatively small audience, as different stations often attract different listeners.

The Importance of Radio

VIEWPOINT

In 2000, Sheila Patricka Dallas, general manager of United Nations Radio in Sierra Leone, a country in West Africa, explained why radio is such a vital technology:

"Radio is cheap to produce and to receive .... There is some TV here in Freetown, but it doesn't reach the whole country. Radio can. In most places, electricity is erratic or even nonexistent. Radios can be powered by batteries or even hand-crank."

Two disc jockeys (DJs) are broadcasting from a digital radio studio in New York City. Music radio stations, where DJs play music with short sections of news and discussion, are extremely popular.

 PROS: CHANGING RADIO BROADCASTS

There are many more radio stations today than in the past, giving listeners more choices. That is especially true for music radio. FM and Internet radio have high-quality sound, which is especially useful for listening to music.

 CONS: CHANGING RADIO BROADCASTS

There are some problems with digital technology. Digital radios are more expensive, and they use more power than conventional radios do. In addition, many areas cannot yet receive digital broadcasts.

CHAPTER 4

Satellites

In the late 1950s, humans traveled into space for the first time, sparking huge excitement around the world. However, other space launches that began around the same time were also very important. Those launches were satellites — small spacecraft that were propelled into orbit around Earth. Satellites play a vital role in modern communications.

By the 1950s, the radio wave spectrum was becoming very crowded. There was not enough space for all the long-distance telephone calls that people wanted to make. One solution to the problem was to use satellites in space, which would act as mirrors to bounce radio waves back to Earth.

Communications Satellites

The first successful satellite, the Soviet *Sputnik 1*, was launched in 1957. It was not a communications satellite, but it broadcast radio signals for

A communications satellite is pictured in orbit above Earth.

22 days as it orbited Earth. Two U.S. satellites launched in 1960 were designed for radio communications. *Echo 1* was a passive satellite. It was a 100-foot-wide (30-meter) plastic balloon that simply acted as a mirror, reflecting radio waves back to Earth. *Courier 1B* was an active satellite. It received radio signals, amplified them, then sent them back to Earth.

The first commercial communications satellite was *Telstar 1*, launched in 1962. It was used for long-distance television transmissions, as well as for carrying telephone calls. More communications satellites soon followed, including another *Telstar* and three *Syncom* satellites. In 1964, the *Syncom 3* satellite was used to transmit live television coverage of the Tokyo Olympic Games across the Pacific Ocean from Japan to the United States.

In 1962, cameras recorded one of the first satellite TV broadcasts. A speech by U.S. President John F. Kennedy was beamed to the *Telstar 1* satellite in space. From there, it was broadcast across Europe.

Building and launching communications satellites was expensive, but countries across the world benefited from them. Satellite communications soon became a global business. In 1964, the International Telecommunications Satellite Consortium (INTELSAT) was established. Eventually, INTELSAT took over ownership of all satellites and began to manage the global communications satellite network.

Satellite Orbits

Satellites can be placed in many different types of orbits. To follow the movement of satellites in most orbits, transmitters and receivers on Earth need tracking devices. There are times when satellites are out of contact. For that reason, communications satellites are often placed in geosynchronous orbit. That is an orbit in which the satellite travels around Earth at the same speed Earth spins. Seen from the ground, the satellite seems to hover in the same spot.

Geosynchronous orbits are very high. Placing a satellite in such an orbit is expensive, and so are the satellites themselves. Satellites in low earth orbit (LEO) are much cheaper because they can be smaller and less powerful. However, an array of LEO satellites is needed for continuous communications.

Televisions and cell phones also use satellites. Networks of LEO satellites make it easy to relay cell phone calls over long distances. Satellite communications are now so advanced that news reporters send broadcast-quality voice reports and videos from almost anywhere in the world, using briefcase-sized transmitters that relay signals to communications satellites.

PROS: COMMUNICATIONS SATELLITES

Communications satellites have made communications truly global. In 1969, a string of satellites beamed live pictures of the first moon landing to nearly every country in the world. Satellite TV has offered people many more choices. Satellite links can carry many more channels than Earth-based television broadcasts can.

CONS: COMMUNICATIONS SATELLITES

Satellites work for only a certain period of time. Once they stop working, they are simply space junk orbiting Earth. There are now so many pieces of space junk that they are a hazard to space missions and to important unpiloted spacecraft.

Communication by satellite makes it possible to get in touch from even the most remote places. This satellite telephone is about 13,000 feet (4,000 meters) above sea level and is on a trail to Mount Everest, a mountain on the border between Nepal and Tibet.

Space Junk

VIEWPOINT

NASA, the U.S. space agency, reported that there are more than 9,000 pieces of space junk orbiting Earth. How dangerous are they?

"[Only the removal of existing large objects from orbit] can prevent future problems .... Although the risk is small, we need to pay attention to this environmental problem."

(NASA report, 2006)

CHAPTER 5

Television

A television set brings a whole range of information and entertainment directly into your home — movies, dramas, news, talk shows, game shows, and many other kinds of programs. Television was first developed in the 1920s and 1930s. By that time, radio was very popular and most homes had a radio. During that period, the first "talking pictures" appeared. Television combined the idea of movies with soundtracks and radio broadcasts.

Inventing Television

Several different people are said to have invented television. Probably the first demonstration of a complete television system was made by a British inventor named John Logie Baird in 1925. Logie Baird used some ideas that had been developed earlier by other people. The most important part of his television was a spinning disk, invented in 1883 by Paul Nipkow of Germany.

Logie Baird's television produced crude and fuzzy pictures. American Philo Farnsworth had an idea for a better system. He built the first demonstration model in 1927. Farnsworth's television was solid state — it had no moving mechanical parts. That allowed it to produce much clearer pictures. The disadvantage was that very bright lights were needed for the camera to get a good picture.

A Russian-born American inventor named Vladimir Zworykin came up

Transmitting Pictures

Television signals contain far more information than a sound signal from the radio or a telephone does. A television image is made up of more than 100,000 picture elements, or pixels, which are tiny dots on the screen. Every second, 25 or 30 images are transmitted. That means the picture signal has to be able to carry up to 3 million pieces of information every second. Sending that much information on a radio wave requires about 600 times more bandwidth than a radio signal does.

with the first television system to be widely used by television companies. In 1923, Zworykin developed a television camera called an iconoscope. It could produce pictures as good as those from Farnsworth's television system without the need for such bright lights.

Black and White

The first television companies formed in the 1930s. One of the first events to be televised was the 1936 Olympics in Berlin. At first, people did not have their own television sets. Instead, televisions were set up in theaters and in large stores, where many people could go to watch them. In the United States, television first attracted wide attention at a huge exhibition called the New York World's Fair in 1939.

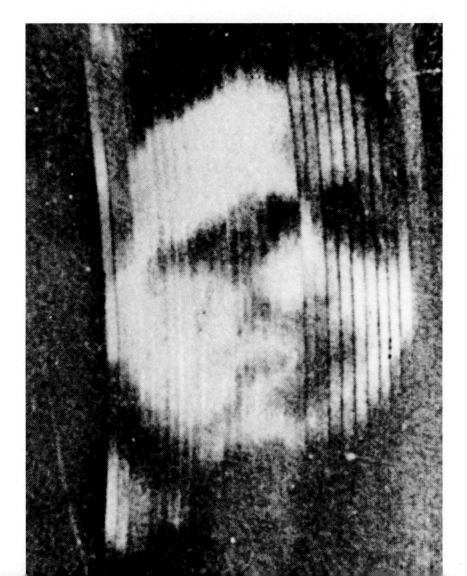

This blurred picture of a face is from what was probably the first public demonstration of television, by John Logie Baird, in 1925.

Television Becomes Popular

After World War II, people in the United States began to buy television sets. In 1945, there were 7,000 TV sets in the whole country; by 1950, there were more than 12 million. In Europe it took longer for television ownership to develop. Most people did not acquire television sets until the 1950s. In the United Kingdom, manufacturers rented televisions to make them more affordable.

The rise of television had a huge impact on movies and radio programs. In the 1930s, motion pictures were hugely popular. Many people would go to the movies three times a week or more. Films with news about recent events, called newsreels, were shown before feature

A group of friends watches television together. In the United States, children and young people watch an average of 28 hours of television per week.

films. Once television became popular, the number of people going to the movies fell and newsreels disappeared. People could now watch the news several times a day on TV. Radio audiences fell, too.

Color TV

John Logie Baird experimented with color television as early as 1928, but color television broadcasting actually began in the United States. After World War II, several U.S. companies developed color TV systems. However, it was not until the 1970s, when other countries besides the United States also began to broadcast in color, that color TV really took off.

Cathode Ray Tubes

Until recently, cathode ray tubes (CRTs) were used for all televisions. A CRT is a large glass tube with no air inside. At one end are three electron guns. That fires a stream of electrons along the tube. That is like a flow of electricity, because electricity is a flow of electrons. The electrons hit a screen at the other end of the CRT. That screen is covered with thousands of tiny dots of phosphor, a substance that lights up when electrons hit it. The phosphor dots are three different colors — red, blue, and green. Each electron gun scans across the screen very fast, lighting up phosphor dots to create the TV picture. A new picture is composed in this way 25 or 30 times per second, so the eye sees a moving image.

 PROS: WATCHING TELEVISION

Television is a powerful way to convey information because pictures have a more immediate impact than sounds or words do. Some studies by scientists show that television programs can improve children's language skills and help in their education.

 CONS: WATCHING TELEVISION

Watching television is a very passive activity. Many people get hooked and watch whatever comes on the screen for hours. Studies suggest that violent television programs and television advertising can affect childrens' behavior. Other studies have found that people who watch a lot of television are less active and more likely to be overweight.

Recording Television

In the 1940s and early 1950s, there was no way to record television programs and edit them. Anything that went wrong in a show simply went out live, sometimes with hilarious results. In one show, for example, an actor playing a character who had been shot and killed in the story crawled off the set while the live action continued around him.

Then, in 1956, a U.S. recording company called Ampex produced the first experimental videotape recorders, which recorded programs directly

A television cameraman records a basketball game on videotape. In the past, high-quality cameras were large and heavy. Today, professional quality television cameras can be handheld.

onto magnetic tape. Until the late 1970s, videotapes were stored and played on large open reels. In the 1970s, the Japanese company Sony introduced the first videocassette. Videocassettes used narrower tape, and the two tape reels were enclosed in a plastic casing. In the 1980s and 1990s, millions of people bought videocassettes to record television programs for home viewing.

At first, film and television companies fought against the introduction of videos. But they soon found that they could make large amounts of money from selling videos of films or programs. Many movies were given new life through sales of videos.

Video Wars

The first videocassette recorders (VCRs) were produced by the Japanese firm Sony in the 1970s. The cassette system Sony used was called Betamax. In 1976, another Japanese company, JVC, produced a different home video system called VHS. The two video systems were not compatible. For several years, the two companies competed, and each tried to persuade the public to choose its system. In the end, VHS became more popular and Betamax disappeared. In the history of communications, there have been several examples of this kind between competing versions of a new technology.

 PROS: VIDEO RECORDING

Videotaping enables programs to be edited before they are broadcast. Programs can also be stored and shown again. Home video recording has made it possible for people to record their favorite TV shows and to rent movies and watch them whenever they want.

 CONS: VIDEO RECORDING

Audiences at movie theaters shrank as people began watching movies on video at home instead. Film companies lost money because people were able to make copies of movies to sell them illegally. Because video footage can be edited, it is sometimes difficult to assess the accuracy of what is being shown. Film directors sometimes complain about the way their movies are edited, shortened, or altered for video and television.

Television Through Cables

Radio waves are ideal for broadcasting television. However, not all places have access to a television transmitter. Cable television began in the United States in the 1950s. It was used to reach remote areas where TV transmissions could not be received. People usually had to pay a monthly fee to receive television via cable. In the 1970s, cable companies began to offer more TV channels. That was possible because cables can carry far more programs than radio waves can. Many people started to buy cable television for the extra channels.

Today, cable companies offer 24-hour news shows. Some channels show only movies, sports, or other themed programs. Cable companies also offer fast Internet connections and inexpensive telephone service.

Satellite TV

Satellite television is another system that offers many channels to viewers. Satellite TV broadcasts are carried by microwaves, which can carry more channels than radio waves. Because communications satellites orbit high above Earth, their transmissions reach a large area. Satellite companies charge customers for the channels that they supply. To stop nonsubscribers with satellite dishes from being able to pick up the

LCD stands for liquid crystal display. LCDs are one of several kinds of flat screens that have replaced CRTs as television screens. The 108-inch (274-centimeter) screen shown here is one of the biggest.

broadcasts, the television signals are encoded, or scrambled. Satellite service providers give customers a decoder to unscramble the signal.

PROS: CABLE AND SATELLITE

In the early days of television, cable channels gave a better quality picture than channels received with a signal from a transmitter. Today, both cable and satellite television offer viewers a far greater choice of channels than ever before. Customers may also get other benefits, such as affordable, high-speed Internet connections.

CONS: CABLE AND SATELLITE

The need to fill airtime on the large number of channels on satellite and cable networks has resulted in many programs of questionable value. For example, many networks sell large blocks of viewing time to businesses that produce "infomercials" designed only to sell products.

Television: Good or Bad?

VIEWPOINT

Experts disagree about the effects that TV has had on people's lives:

"Adolescents who watched more than one hour a day of television … were roughly four times more likely to commit aggressive acts toward other people later in their lives than those who watched less than one hour."

(Results of a 2002 study led by Jeffrey Johnson of Columbia University, New York, and reported by Mark Sappenfield in the Christian Science Monitor)

"At its best, TV can educate and inspire. High-quality documentaries offer insights into history that no book can equal. Nature programs … take us to places many of us will never be able to visit."

(From the book The Elephant in the Living Room, by Dimitri A. Christakis and Frederick J. Zimmerman, experts in child development)

Going Digital

As computers have developed and become increasingly important, various parts of the television process have been digitized. In television cameras, charge-coupled devices (CCDs) record the brightness patterns of a scene as millions of individual pixels, rather than as a continuously changing signal. Digital processors turn the raw picture and sound information into a television signal. Optical disks such as DVDs store video signals digitally and can be used to play them back. The flat LCD screens and plasma displays that have replaced CRTs also work digitally.

In the early 21st century, cable and satellite companies began to broadcast some programs digitally. A digital television signal can be compressed before it is transmitted, so a digital signal takes up less bandwidth than an analog one. That means that more channels can be broadcast. There is also space for interactive TV, where viewers can send messages or choose what they watch from "on-demand" platforms.

Around the world, most major television broadcasters still broadcast analog programs. That is because millions of television viewers have television sets that cannot receive digital signals. Most of the more developed countries will change over completely to digital broadcasts in the near future. The United States was the first to do so, switching over to digital broadcasting in 2009. Japan was to make the switch by 2011, countries in the European Union by 2012, and Australia by 2013.

 PROS: DIGITAL TV

Digital televisions give better sound and picture quality. Each digital channel also takes up less bandwidth, so more channels can be transmitted. That gives viewers more choice.

 CONS: DIGITAL TV

The switch to digital TV will mean that analog television sets will not work without modification. Anyone who wants to receive digital TV will have to either buy a new television, or get a digital converter box.

HDTV

Since the 1960s, the pictures on television screens have been made up of either 525 or 625 lines. However, digital signals can carry more information in the same bandwidth, so digital transmissions can be better quality. Some TV programs are now made in high definition (HD). Those HD images are almost 10 times more detailed than normal television pictures. Some satellite and cable television broadcasts are already HD. There are also many HDTV sets now for sale, usually with large plasma screens. However, until there is a complete switch to digital, many programs will still be available only in standard definition television broadcasts.

The CBS3 television news studio in Philadelphia was one of the first stations to produce its broadcasts only in high definition.

CHAPTER 6

The Internet

The Internet has had a bigger impact on communications than anything since printing. Most people began to be aware of the Internet only in the 1990s. But it began in the 1960s, when a group of scientists tried to tackle the problem of getting different computers to talk to one another.

The First Networks

In 1960, American computer scientist Joseph Licklider popularized the idea that computers could one day be connected through a world network of high-speed links. In 1962, Licklider went to work for the U.S. Department of Defense Advanced Research Projects Agency (ARPA). He led a group in finding ways to send information between different computers. In 1969, the group connected four computers at several research centers in the United States. That network, called the Advanced Research Projects Agency Network (ARPANET), was the first step on the road to the Internet.

Information Packets

The crucial technology at the center of the ARPANET was packet switching. That was a way of sending information from one computer in a network to another. Packet switching has important advantages over other ways of sending information. Because each packet is short, the connection between one point in a network and another has to be open for only a short time for the

Packet Switching

In packet switching, a piece of information being sent through a network is divided into small pieces, or packets. Each packet has a "label" on it saying where it is from, where it is going, and where the packet fits into the overall piece of information. The packets are sent separately through the network. At each connection in the network, there is a computer called a router. Its job is simply to send packets from one place to the next. Different packets may take different routes from sender to receiver. The packets are put back in the right order as they arrive at their final address.

packet to travel along it. A break in communication does not mean that the whole message has to be sent again. Other advantages of breaking information up is that packets can travel by different routes, and packets from many different messages can use the network at the same time.

Friends meet at an Internet café. Today, the Internet is part of everyday life for vast numbers of people around the world.

Connecting Networks

The ARPANET soon added more computer centers to its network. Other groups also set up their own networks using the packet switching idea. By the 1970s, there were several networks all working independently of one another. Connecting those networks was a problem because the computers used different systems for talking to one another. Robert E. Kahn at DARPA and Vinton Cerf of Stanford University in California came up with an idea to solve that problem. They suggested that whatever system was used within a network, when networks communicated with one another, they would use a common set of rules. Kahn, Cerf, and others developed a protocol, or set of rules, called Transmission Control Protocol/Internet Protocol (TCP/IP). It became the common language of the Internet in 1983, and it is still used today.

You've Got Mail

E-mail was one of the first ways the Internet was used and it is still one of the most popular. E-mail was used before the Internet began to develop commercially in the 1990s, but only in a very limited way. In 1971, Ray Tomlinson, who worked on the ARPANET, came up with the e-mail address format that we still use today: "sender@address." Today, there are about 1.3 billion e-mail users worldwide. Nearly 2.5 million e-mails are sent on the Internet every second.

How E-mail Works

Most individuals are connected to the Internet through an Internet service provider (ISP). A server, a large, fast computer at the ISP, has a "mailbox" for each person's e-mail. When you send an e-mail to a friend, it goes first to your mailbox, then travels through the Internet to your friend's mailbox. To pick up the message, your friend connects to his or her mailbox on the ISP server, and looks in his or her in-box. Your friend can either read the e-mails without moving them from the mailbox, or download the e-mails to his or her computer.

 PROS: E-MAIL

E-mail was probably the greatest benefit of the early Internet. E-mail has two advantages over the telephone. First, e-mail doesn't have to be looked at as soon as it arrives — people can choose their own time. Second, e-mails are written. That means they can be used to send complex information, such as facts and figures.

 CONS: E-MAIL

The biggest problem with e-mail is spam — unwanted e-mails that are sent to thousands or even millions of people at once. More than 70 percent of all e-mail is spam. Some is advertising and is simply annoying. However, other spam e-mails contain viruses or programs that can damage a computer or steal a user's personal information, such as his or her financial data and account numbers.

Instant Messaging

Instant messaging was first used in the 1960s, but it did not become a common part of the Internet until the mid-1990s. When someone logs on to his or her instant messaging service, he or she can see which friends or contacts are also online. The person can type a text message to any of those people, and it will appear immediately on the other person's computer screen. The two people can continue to chat online, with messages appearing on the screen as they are typed. Some instant messaging providers also offer extra features, such as group chatting or online conferencing using sound and video.

In instant messaging, two people can have a real-time conversation just as if they were on the telephone except the conversation is written instead of spoken.

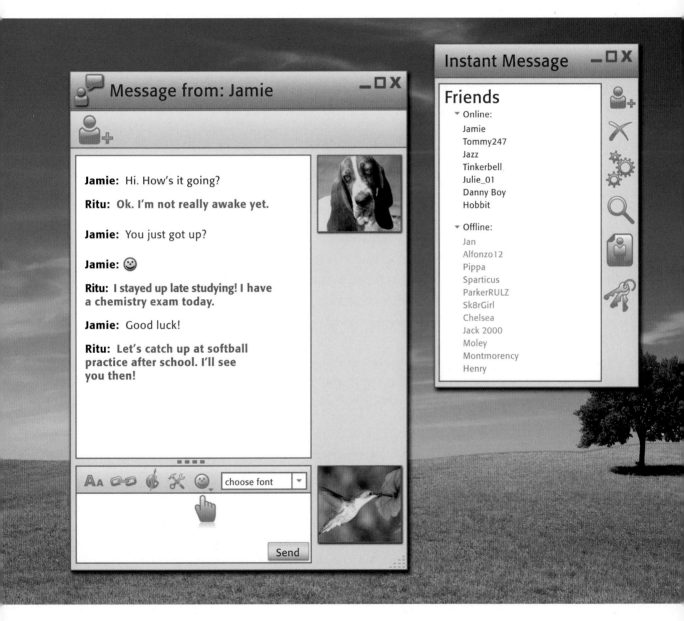

Message from: Jamie _□X

Jamie: Hi. How's it going?

Ritu: Ok. I'm not really awake yet.

Jamie: You just got up?

Jamie: ☺

Ritu: I stayed up late studying! I have a chemistry exam today.

Jamie: Good luck!

Ritu: Let's catch up at softball practice after school. I'll see you then!

choose font

Send

Instant Message _□X

Friends

▼ Online:

Jamie
Tommy247
Jazz
Tinkerbell
Julie_01
Danny Boy
Hobbit

▼ Offline:

Jan
Alfonzo12
Pippa
Sparticus
ParkerRULZ
Sk8rGirl
Chelsea
Jack 2000
Moley
Montmorency
Henry

Changing Use

In the 1970s, the invention of microprocessors made it possible to build smaller, less expensive computers. By the 1980s, people were beginning to buy personal computers (PCs) to use either for work or at home. When PCs first appeared, using the Internet involved writing computer commands. It was not user-friendly. In the late 1980s and early 1990s, the Internet became much more accessible to people.

The World Wide Web

Today, most people use the Internet by exploring the World Wide Web, the vast collection of web sites and pages that are visible online. The idea of the Web was developed at the European Organization for Nuclear Research (CERN) in Switzerland by a British scientist, Tim Berners-Lee. He invented hypertext, a way of linking one piece of information to another on the Internet by clicking on a word or picture. Berners-Lee built all the tools needed to create web pages. In 1991, he put a notice on the Internet explaining the World Wide Web and inviting other people to become involved. Those were the first web pages.

With the development of the World Wide Web, the Internet became much more user-friendly. In the 1990s, the Internet turned into a commercial network, and the first ISPs appeared. Web browsers such as Mosaic made it easier for people to use the network, and search engines such as Yahoo!, AltaVista, and Google helped users find information.

Internet: Good or Bad?

VIEWPOINT

This summary of the advantages and the drawbacks of the Internet comes from an essay written in 2000 by Bill Gates, cofounder of Microsoft Corporation:

"Some optimists view the Internet as humanity's greatest invention … At the other extreme, pessimists think the Internet will result in … the death of privacy, and a decline in values and social standards. If history is any guide, neither side of these arguments will be proved right."

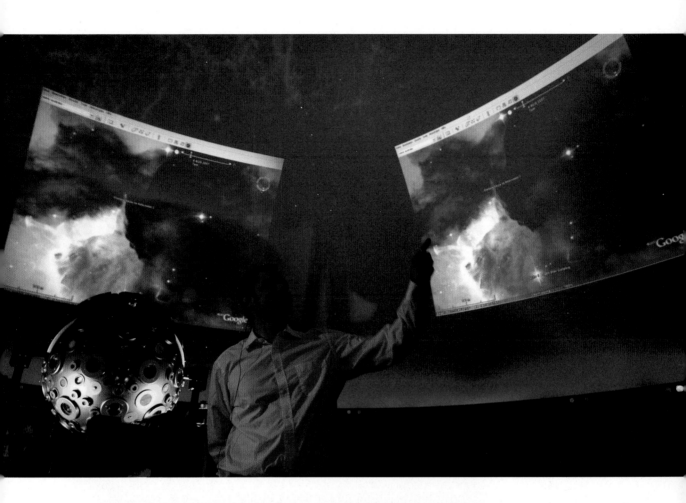

 PROS: INTERNET

Scientific researchers were using the Internet to share ideas and results long before it became popular. As more people connected to the Internet, everyone from journalists to schoolchildren began to use it to find information they wanted to know.

 CONS: INTERNET

Information from the Internet is not always reliable. Some web sites have information that is inaccurate. Others give only one side of an argument, or information that is deliberately false.

The Google search engine was launched on the Internet in 1998. It quickly became popular for its ability to give relevant search results. Today, Google is far more than just a search engine. In 2007, the company launched Google Sky — a virtual telescope that allows Internet users to view 100 million stars and 200 million galaxies.

Boom and Bust

The number of computers connected to the Internet grew rapidly. In 1990, there were about 300,000. By 1999, that number had risen to more than 56 million. Until the mid-1990s, the Internet was run by universities and research organizations. Those organizations did not allow the Internet to be used for making money. Starting in 1994, however, commercial companies began to take over the Internet.

Hundreds of new Internet companies sprang up. At first those "dot-com" companies were very successful. However, making money on the Internet turned out to be no easier than making money in any other business. In 2000, the dot-com industry collapsed, and many companies went bankrupt. Some dot-com companies, such as Google, eBay, and Amazon, survived the collapse and went on to become large businesses. New dot-com companies such as YouTube and Facebook have also developed since 2000 and have had great success. Millions of other businesses use the Internet as a way to advertise and sell their products and services.

Access to the Internet

VIEWPOINT

The Internet is increasingly important — but large numbers of people do not have access to such technology. People in richer countries have more opportunities to use the Internet than people in poorer ones do:

"The importance of the Internet in a teenager's life increases with every day that goes by. Teenagers are starting to use the Internet in a myriad of ways, which range from doing schoolwork to transporting themselves halfway around the world."
(David Thelen, U.S. high school student)

"Globalization, as defined by rich people like us, is a very nice thing .... [Y]ou are talking about the Internet, you are talking about cell phones, you are talking about computers. That doesn't affect two-thirds of the people of the world."
(Former U.S. President Jimmy Carter)

Making the World Smaller

The end of the dot-com boom did not stop the growth of the Internet. In 2008, there were nearly 600 million computers connected to the Internet and nearly 1.5 billion Internet users. That is almost a quarter of the world's population.

Today, people can do a huge variety of things on the Internet. They can listen to music or watch television, read the news, meet new people, play games with a group of friends, shop, book a vacation, get tickets for a concert, or take a virtual trip around the world. The Internet can also be used in more serious ways. People in some businesses use it to work from home. People campaigning against injustice or in politics can make their voice heard regionally, or around the world. People with a medical problem can get in touch with others who have the same illness to share information and offer support. Many people pay their bills and manage their bank accounts online. In addition, there is information on the Internet on every subject imaginable, all of it available in just minutes with a click of the mouse.

Fans of the British rock group the Arctic Monkeys made a MySpace web site where people could hear the group's music. The site helped make the band very popular even before they released an album.

The Internet and Wireless

The most recent development in Internet communications is wireless connection. That involves using high-frequency radio signals to send information to and from a receiver connected to the Internet. Wireless links can be used in homes and offices to connect a group of computers to the Internet. In many towns and cities there are also "hotspots" where any computer with a wireless link can connect to the Internet. More recently, it has become possible for a computer to use a cell phone as a direct connection to the Internet.

Grid Computing

The Internet is a great way to share information around the world. But single computers do not have enough memory or processing power for some jobs. To solve that problem, scientists are turning to a new kind of network, called grid computing. Computers on a grid interconnect to share memory and processing power, turning them into one vast, powerful mega-computer. One example of grid computing is the WISDOM project, which began in 2005. That medical project has been using grid computing to examine the structures of 1 million chemicals, to see whether any might make good antimalarial drugs. In just three weeks, the list of chemicals was reduced to 30 likely candidates.

These computers at CERN in Switzerland are part of a grid network that enables them to share information with scientists around the world.

PROS: GLOBAL COMMUNICATIONS

The Internet has given many people a voice. For example, when the United States and its allies invaded Iraq in 2003, a blogger writing under the name Salam Pax, in Baghdad, discussed the war from an Iraqi point of view. In 2007, news of mass protests in Myanmar reached the rest of the world through photos and short videos sent over the Internet by people in that country.

 CONS: GLOBAL COMMUNICATIONS

The Internet has created opportunities for many new kinds of crime. Criminals have found ways to steal banking and business information. A common crime is identity theft. A criminal steals personal information, such as someone's name and Social Security number, and uses it to pretend to be that person and defraud him or her. Some people use the Internet to target young people. They join social networks and pretend to make friends. They actually want to do harm. All young people using the Internet need to be aware of such dangers.

Safety Rules on the Internet

- Do not reveal your home address, phone number, school name, or any personal information.
- Do not arrange to meet someone you know only online, and don't send strangers photos.
- Remember that people do not always tell the truth on the Internet and are not always who they seem.
- Always tell parents or teachers if you get nasty messages.

CHAPTER 7

Cell Phones

Cell phones became hugely popular in the 1990s. However, cell phone technology has been developing slowly since the 1920s. Probably the earliest "mobile" telephones were installed in 1926 on passenger trains in Germany. By the 1950s, a few radiotelephones were being used in cars. Those early cell phones worked by sending out a strong radio signal to a central radio transceiver, a combined transmitter and receiver. The transceiver picked up the signals and sent them through the normal telephone system. The phones were large and heavy, and needed powerful batteries.

A major problem with early radiotelephones was that very few could be used in a particular area. That was because only a small part of the total radio wave spectrum could be used for radiotelephones without interfering with other radio transmissions.

The Cellular Idea

The breakthrough idea that eventually led to modern cell phones came from the United States in 1947. Two engineers at Bell Laboratories, Douglas Ring and Rae Young, came up with a way for a large number of phones to communicate with the telephone system using only a small number of radio channels. Their idea was for a network of radio transceivers, each of which would pick up and send signals within a fairly small area, called a cell. Each cell was six-sided. That hexagonal shape worked best because the cells fit together neatly, like the cells in a honeycomb. Each transceiver sent and received messages only over the area of its cell. When a phone reached the edge of a particular cell, the call would be handed over to the next cell. Rae and Young determined that they could avoid interference between cells using just seven different radio channels. Those seven channels could be used in a repeating pattern over a large area.

Walkie-Talkies

During World War II, armed forces developed lightweight two-way radios that became known as walkie-talkies. The first U.S. walkie-talkie was a device called the Handie-Talkie. It weighed about 5 pounds (2.3 grams) and was about 14 inches (36 centimeters) long. English engineer Donald Hings developed a larger walkie-talkie for the British and Canadian armies around 1941. The research that went into walkie-talkies contributed to the development of cell phones.

A police officer in Hong Kong uses a walkie-talkie to communicate with colleagues.

The First Cell Phone

When Ring and Young came up with the cellular idea, the technology to make it work was unavailable. Keeping track of many different cell phones and transferring signals for each one as they moved out of one cell and into the next required the processing power of a computer. However, the few computers that existed in 1946 were large and took up a whole room.

The development of transistors and computers after World War II meant that, by the 1960s, cellular technology was possible. In 1970, Amos Joel, another engineer at Bell Laboratories, developed a method for automatically transferring a cell phone call from one cell in the network to another. In 1973, Martin Cooper, an engineer at the U.S. company Motorola, demonstrated the first truly mobile cell phone.

Battery Technology

The weight and size of early cell phones was largely due to the battery. Many early handsets had a separate battery pack. In the 1990s, new batteries were made with a combination of nickel and a metal alloy. Those small nickel-metal hydride (NiMH) batteries provided plenty of power. Modern cell phones now use even smaller batteries, made from the metal lithium. The latest lithium polymer batteries are very slim and can be shaped to fit the phone casing.

Setting Up Networks

U.S. scientists were the first to develop cellular technology. However, when it came to establishing cellular networks, other countries were ahead of the United States. The first commercial cell phone network was launched in Tokyo, Japan, in 1979. In 1981, the Nordic Mobile Telephone system, which covered Finland, Denmark, Norway, and Sweden, began operating. By 1985, more than 200,000 people were using that network, making it the biggest in the world at the time.

⊕ PROS: EARLY MOBILE PHONES

Although early mobile phones had their limitations, they showed that mobile technology could work. Cell phones are especially useful in places such as Scandinavia, where there are few people spread over a large area and laying telephone cables to every home is expensive.

⊖ CONS: EARLY MOBILE PHONES

Early mobile phones were large, heavy, and expensive. The first commercial Motorola phone weighed about 1 pound (450 grams) and cost $3,500. That phone also had a very short battery life, often having only enough power for 10 minutes of continuous use.

Second Generation

Cell phone technology improved very quickly. In the 1990s, new digital networks were set up that were a great improvement over the earlier analog networks. A second generation of cell phones appeared that were smaller, lighter, and cheaper than the early so-called bricks. They had a screen, a telephone directory, and some simple games. With those improvements, cell phones suddenly mushroomed in popularity, especially in Japan and the United States.

Around the world, antennas such as this one pick up microwave signals from cell phones and feed them into the conventional telephone network.

Text Messaging

One of the biggest surprises of the second-generation phone systems was the success of text messaging. GSM, which was the phone system set up in Europe, included a feature called short messaging service (SMS). That allowed phone users to send brief text messages with fewer than 160 characters. To keep to the limit, people shortened words and phrases, or replaced them with symbols.

 PROS: TEXTING

Text messages are simple to send. They are cheaper than phone calls, and the person receiving the text can respond when he or she can.

 CONS: TEXTING

Text messaging can become addictive and can stop people from learning or working effectively. Many accidents have been caused by people texting while driving.

Many cell phones today have sophisticated features, such as Internet access and built-in cameras.

VIEWPOINT

The Dangers of Cell Phones

After many years of research into the safety of cell phones, some experts believe they pose little or no danger to human health, while others take the opposite view:

"Mobile phones, cordless phones, and cordless base stations next to beds are safe, pose no risk of cancer to adult users, and do not cause headaches or sleeping problems."
(Report in the British Medical Journal, 2008)

"Children and teenagers are five times more likely to get brain cancer if they use mobile phones, startling new research indicates."
(2008 article in The Independent about a Swedish research report)

Third-Generation Networks

In the 21st century, cell phone networks have changed once again. Third-generation (3G) phone networks offer far more than just phone calls. The phone signals are greatly compressed, which leaves space to use some bandwidth for other purposes. People can send and receive e-mails, surf the Internet, and even watch streaming videos on their cell phones. 3G phones also have many more features, such as color screens, MP3 players, and cameras. Many have a Global Positioning System (GPS), a satellite navigation system that enables users to know their position anywhere on Earth. Some phones have a keyboard rather than only a number pad. Those "smart phones" are like minicomputers.

 PROS: CELL PHONES

Cell phones have became an essential part of many people's lives. In emergency situations, cell phones have frequently made it possible to call for help. For example, in 2007, three climbers who fell on Mount Hood in Oregon were rescued when other climbers with them used their cell phones to alert rescue services.

CONS: CELL PHONES

Cell phones are very useful, but it is important to know when to turn them off. Businesspeople often feel that they must keep their cell phones on all the time. However, always being available to receive calls can make people very stressed. The ringtones of cell phones and overhearing phone conversations can annoy or distract others in places such as theaters or trains. Cell phones may also be a health risk. For example, some scientific studies suggest that using cell phones for several years can significantly increase the risk of getting brain or ear cancers. However, other scientific studies show no health risks from cell phone use.

An X-ray of a cell phone shows the complex electronic circuits inside.

What's Inside a Cell Phone?

A cell phone packs an enormous amount of technology into a small space. Like a conventional telephone, the cell phone needs a microphone and a speaker. It also needs a battery, an antenna to pick up radio signals, and a screen to display information. However, the most important parts of the phone are the electronics. There are several different electronic parts:

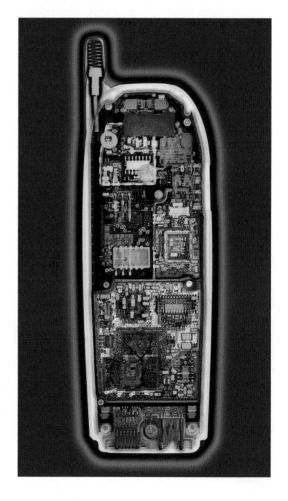

- **Analog to digital (A to D) microchips** The signals coming from the microphone and going to the speakers are analog, but the signals transmitted and received are digital. A to D microchips convert the signals back and forth.
- **Digital signal processor (DSP)** The signals going in and out of the phone are highly compressed. The DSP does the compressing and decompressing.
- **Radio frequency (RF) chips** These produce the radio waves that carry the phone signals. An amplifier chip makes the signals stronger.

- **Memory chips** Memory chips are used to store phone numbers and other information.
- **Microprocessor** The microprocessor is the brain of the phone. It broadcasts the phone's unique identity number, so that the system knows where the phone is. The microprocessor also knows the radio frequencies of the nearest cells and monitors the strongest signal at each moment to secure the best reception.

 PROS: CELLULAR REVOLUTION

The cell phone brings together most of the modern communications media, including radio, television, e-mail, and the World Wide Web. Many cell phones can also be used to record sounds and music, take pictures, and make short videos.

 CONS: CELLULAR REVOLUTION

Although cell phones are expensive, they do not last long. Manufacturers are always releasing new phones with more features. The result is that billions of phones are thrown away each year. Phones form a significant part of the millions of tons of electronic waste, or e-waste, thrown away each year — about 55 million tons globally.

Environmental Impact

VIEWPOINT

In an article for BBC News, science and nature reporter Mark Kinver wrote about research conducted by Dr. Dylan Gwynn Jones of the University of Wales on the environmental impact of mobile phones:

"As with all electronic equipment, mobile phones contain a range of substances that are harmful if the devices are not disposed of properly. Heavy metals such as mercury, lead, and cadmium are present within [cell] phones, especially older models."

CHAPTER 8

Looking to the Future

In this book, we have examined the various kinds of communications technology separately, but all those technologies are interconnected. The first telephones used telegraph wires to send signals. Television broadcasts are transmitted using radio waves. Computers connect to the Internet through the telephone or cable network.

Cell phones are the essence of modern communications. A modern cell phone can replace nearly all other modern communications devices. People use it as a telephone, a radio, and a music player. Cell phones can be used to surf the Internet and pinpoint the user's location using GPS. Some cell phones can even be used to watch television programs.

Faster and Freer

The speed of communications will continue to get faster. Early Internet connections were narrowband — they could only send information slowly (about 54,000 "bits" of information per second). Today's Internet connections are broadband — they can send up to 8 million bits of information every second. The next generation of cell phones (4G) will work at broadband speeds, while new Internet connections will be more than 12 times faster than current broadband speeds. In some countries, ultrafast broadband links are already available. The future will also be

PCFs

Photonic crystal fibers (PCFs) could be the communications cables of the future. PCFs are made of silica glass, but instead of being solid, they have very tiny channels along their length. The channels filter out all frequencies of light except one, which is carried down the length of the fiber. That allows them to carry much more information than conventional optical fibers can. PCFs can also be used to make an extremely bright kind of laser, called a sunlight laser. Sunlight lasers produce very brief pulses of light that are 10,000 times brighter than the sun. A laser that bright could be used to increase the amount of data carried by optical fibers.

wireless. Internet "hotspot" connections are already available for laptop computers to use in many places. In the future, wireless access will be the norm rather than the exception.

 PROS: FUTURE TECHNOLOGY

In the future, technology will make communications even simpler and more convenient. Combining several types of communication into one device will mean that people will not have to buy separate telephones, televisions, computers, radios, and so on. That will make keeping in touch even easier and more affordable.

 CONS: FUTURE TECHNOLOGY

Building good communications networks can be very expensive. It is hard for less-developed countries to afford such networks. That difference in "connectedness" between rich and poor countries has been called the digital divide. Since 1999, the digital divide has narrowed a little. However, as more new technology is introduced, the divide could widen once more.

JEREMY BURROUGHES
Inventor

The Future Is Plastic

A new technology that will change communications in the future is microchips made from polymers, or plastics. That technology is already being used to make plastic electronic display screens that are thin, tough, and flexible. If the screens can be made flexible enough to be rolled up or folded, a cell phone with a roll-up screen could replace our current communications devices.

In the future, fewer books and magazines will likely be printed. Instead, people may read books, newspapers, and other documents

A test version of a television screen was made using plastic electronics. The screen is only 0.08 inches (2 millimeters) thick.

electronically, using a digital reader. That is a device that can store printed material in its memory, and display it on a screen for reading. The latest digital readers use plastic electronics for their screens. It will not be long before those kinds of readers are flexible enough to be rolled up as easily as a magazine or a newspaper is.

The Internet in Space

As part of its plans for space missions to the moon and Mars, NASA, the U.S. space agency, is developing an interplanetary communications network — a "space Internet." Currently, NASA technicians design a new communications system for each space mission they plan. Now they are working on a communications system that has the same basic rules for every space probe and satellite. Every spacecraft will eventually be part of a vast communications network spread out over space.

 PROS: ELECTRONIC COMMUNICATIONS

The amount of information available to us through different media grows day by day. A very useful development for the future would be to find ways of filtering the content we receive to avoid information overload. Intelligent computers might well be able to do that. They could search for information in a much more sophisticated way than today's search engines can and present only the most useful results.

 CONS: ELECTRONIC COMMUNICATIONS

We already rely heavily on electronic communications, and in the future, we will use them even more. But our reliance on electronics means that if they become damaged, there could be a complete communications blackout. That could cause huge disruptions all over the world. Solar flares are one of the potential threats. A solar flare is a massive explosion on the sun's surface that blasts out clouds of electrically-charged particles, called a proton storm. A large flare can produce a proton storm that washes over Earth. The particles do not hurt people or animals, but they can damage all kinds of electronics. The results of such a storm could be disastrous.

GLOSSARY

alloy A material formed from a mixture of metals

amplifier An electronic device that boosts an electrical signal, making it strong enough to be sent farther

amplitude The height of a radio wave

amplitude modulation (AM) A radio signal in which the carrier wave is modified by changing its amplitude

analog An electrical signal or wave that varies continuously

bandwidth The amount of information that can be sent along a communications channel; a high-bandwidth channel can carry a lot of information

binary number A number made up of only 0s and 1s. In binary code, one is 1, two is 10, three is 11, four is 100, and so on

broadband A type of fast Internet connection

carrier wave A high-frequency radio wave that is used to carry information

cell An area where cell phones all connect to a particular transmitter

charge-coupled device (CCD) A grid of light-sensitive detectors in a television camera that are used to record images

circuit board A thin board with a number of electronic components on it

compress To make smaller or more compact

diaphragm In a microphone, a thin metal plate that can vibrate

digital An electrical signal or wave that varies in steps, rather than continuously

dot-com company A business that buys and sells products and services via the Internet

electromagnetic radiation A whole range of similar waves or rays, including light, radio waves, microwaves, infrared, ultraviolet, and X-rays

electron A tiny, negatively charged part of an atom; electricity is a flow of electrons

frequency The number of radio waves produced per second

frequency modulation (FM) A radio signal in which the carrier wave is modified by changing its frequency

geosynchronous orbit An orbit in which a satellite travels around Earth at the same speed Earth spins; satellites seem to hover in the same spot in the sky when viewed from Earth

Global Positioning System (GPS) A system of satellites orbiting Earth that are used for accurate navigation; someone with a GPS handset can use information from satellites to find his or her position almost anywhere on Earth

grid computing A computing network that allows computers around the world to share not just information, but also programs and computing

hertz (Hz) A measure of frequency; one hertz is equal to one cycle (vibration) per second

high-definition television (HDTV) Television broadcasts with better-quality pictures than ordinary TV

high-frequency Describes waves that vibrate back and forth very quickly (more than 3 million times per second)

hypertext Text containing words that have links to other related pieces of information

integrated circuit An electronic circuit in which the transistors, diodes, and other components are all fitted on to a single small "chip" of semiconductor material

Internet service provider (ISP) A company that provides people with a connection to the Internet

liquid crystal display (LCD) A type of flat-screen display containing materials called liquid crystals, which change properties when an electric current flows through them

low earth orbit (LEO) An orbit less than 600 miles (970 kilometers) above Earth's surface

low-frequency Describes waves that vibrate back and forth relatively slowly (less than 300,000 times per second)

magnetic tape Plastic tape that is coated with a layer of tiny magnetic particles and that can be used to store recorded sound or video

microchip An integrated circuit

microprocessor A microchip that contains all the components of a central processing unit, which is the brain of a cell phone

microwaves Electromagnetic waves that have a higher frequency (more energy) than radio waves do, but a lower frequency (less energy) than infrared waves do

modulation When a sound signal is used to modify, or change, a carrier wave so that the wave carries the information in the sound signal

Morse code A code in which letters are represented by a series of dots (short pulses) and dashes (longer pulses)

multiplexing Sending several messages at the same time along the same circuit or channel

obsolete Describes something that is out of date and no longer used

optical fiber A thin, flexible strand of glass that can be used to carry information as pulses of laser light

outsourcing A business practice used to reduce costs by basing parts of the business — call centers, for example — in a country where rates of pay are lower than in the home country of that company

packet switching Sending messages as short packets of information, which are put back together at their destination

patent A grant awarded by a government that gives an inventor ownership of his or her invention

phosphor A substance that lights up when it is hit by electrons

pixel A picture element — a tiny dot or square of just one color or shade that forms part of an image

GLOSSARY

plasma Very hot, electrically charged gas

radio valve An electronic device made from a glass tube containing one or more electrodes (wires carrying an electric current)

radio wave A radio-frequency electromagnetic wave

receiver A device that receives radio or other communications signals

satellite An object that orbits a planet

semaphore A signaling system in which letters or words are represented by positions of two "arms" on top of a tower, or by flags

semiconductor A material such as silicon or gallium, which is not a metal but can conduct electricity in certain circumstances

server A powerful computer, or a program running on a computer, that offers services on the Internet or another network

signal Information carried by a varying electric current, or by variations of a laser light beam

silica glass A hard, clear, high-quality type of glass

spectrum A range of different wavelengths of sound or other electromagnetic radiation

telecommunication Any system of communication at a distance

telegraph A system of sending messages using pulses of electricity along wires

transceiver A combined transmitter and receiver

transistor A semiconductor device that can act either as an amplifier or a switch

transmitter A device that sends out radio or other communications signals

type In printing, type is printed letters and numbers

virus In computing, a program that can reproduce itself and is designed to corrupt or destroy information on a computer's hard drive

wavelength The distance between two peaks of a wave

Web browser A kind of computer software that allows people to look at text, images, videos, music, games, and other information on Internet web sites

World Wide Web A computer network of Internet sites that offer text, graphics, sound, and animated resources through the hypertext transfer protocol

FURTHER INFORMATION

WEB SITES

www.computerhistory.org
The Computer History Museum in Mountain View, California, offers virtual exhibits about the artifacts and stories of the information age.

www.fcc.gov/cgb/kidszone
The Federal Communications Commission (FCC), which regulates telecommunications in the United States, offers a variety of interesting web sites on the history of communications.

www.fcc.gov/omd/history/radio
Radio Pioneers has information about breakthroughs in radio communications.

www.fcc.gov/omd/history/tv
Television Technology tells the story of the development of television.

www.marconiusa.org
The web site of the Guglielmo Marconi Foundation, a museum in Bedford, New Hampshire, offers information about the history of radio broadcasting.

www.museum.tv
The web site of the Museum of Broadcast Communications, located in Chicago, collects, preserves, and presents content from the history of radio and television broadcasting.

www.paleycenter.org
The web site of the Paley Center for Media, with locations in New York and Los Angeles, offers virtual exhibits that consider the cultural, creative, and social significance of television and radio.

www.privateline.com/TelephoneHistory/History 1.htm
Tom Farley's Telephone History explains details about the telephone and its history.

www.warriorsofthe.net/movie.html
Warriors of the Net explains how "packets" of information move about on the Internet.

BOOKS

Agar, John. *Constant Touch: A Brief History of the Mobile Phone.* Icon Books (2003)

Aronson, Mark. *Bill Gates*. Viking Juvenile (2008)

Cox, Michael. *The Knowledge: The Incredible Internet.* Scholastic (2002)

Goldsmith, Dr. Mike. *Scientists Who Made History: John Logie Baird.* Hodder Wayland (2003)

Haugen, Hayley Mitchell. *Internet Safety*. Greenhaven Press (2008)

Imbimbo, Anthony. *Steve Jobs: The Brilliant Mind Behind Apple*. Gareth Stevens Publishing (2009)

Kent, Peter. *Navigators: Technology.* Kingfisher (2009)

Niemi, Robert. *History in the Media: Film and Television*. ABC-CLIO (2006)

Ross, Stewart. *Scientists Who Made History: Alexander Graham Bell.* Hodder Wayland (2001)

Woodford, Chris. *Communications and Computers.* Facts on File (2004)

Woods, Michael, and Mary B. Woods. *The History of Communication*. Lerner Books (2005)

Zannos, Susan. *Guglielmo Marconi and Radio Waves*. Mitchell Lane (2004)

INDEX

Page numbers in **BOLD** refer to illustrations and charts.

About the Author
Andrew Solway has written more than
60 books for children, including titles on
science, history, geography, and books
for early readers. He won a U.K. Literacy
Association Award in 2004.

About the Consultant
Bill Thompson is a technology journalist,
writer, and consultant. He writes for the
BBC News web site, *Focus* magazine,
and others, and appears weekly on
Digital Planet on BBC World Service.